PROBLEM PAGE

ME AND MY FAMILY

JILLIAN POWELL

SEA-TO-SEA

Mankato Collingwood London

Problem Page
Me and my family

Relationships with your family are often difficult. You can't choose your family, and sometimes they're not easy to live with! But who can you share your problems with? The letters, emails, and texts in this book are all from young people who have chosen to confide in friends or write to an advice column. A few have only told their diaries…

★ He'll never be my dad 6
Ryan is tired of his stepdad always bossing him around. Who does he think he is anyway?

★ I can't live up to my brother 8
Conor is fed up that his brother is better than him at everything.

★ I feel caught in the middle 10
It's been three months since Hannah's parents split up, and her mom never stops talking about her dad's new girlfriend. How can Hannah keep her happy?

★ I have to look after my mom 12
Kyle's mom is sick and he has to look after her. But what will happen to them if Kyle gets sick?

★ I still miss grandma 14
Leanne's grandma died six months ago, and Leanne still misses her.

★ I don't like the way he looks at me 16
Sasha's mom's boyfriend makes Sasha uncomfortable. She doesn't like some of the things he says. How can she make him stop?

★ We argue all the time

Kelly's mom is driving her nuts. She is always nagging her and they are always arguing about something. It never used to be like this.

18

★ Mom doesn't have time for me now

Ever since her new baby sister was born, Bethany has been pushed out of everything. Things were much better before the baby was born.

20

★ I can't help wondering about my real mom

Martin has always known he was adopted, but lately he's been thinking about his birth parents. What would it be like to meet them?

22

★ I get no privacy

Sharing a room with her sister is really getting on Leila's nerves. It's not fair!

24

★ They are always making me do chores

Craig's parents treat him like a little kid even though he's 14! How can he get them to see he's grown up now?

26

★ Glossary

★ Websites

28

★ Index

29

30

Dear reader

The postal addresses used in this book have all been changed to fictitious places. The email addresses have also been censored. All the photographs are posed by models.

He'll never be my dad

December 12

Maggie's advice column
Total magazine
Hobert

Dear Maggie,

My stepdad Tony bosses us around like he owns the place. He is really strict and makes up stupid rules that he puts on a board in the kitchen. He won't even let me go to the movies with my friends any more. When we complain to Mom she always takes his side. It really annoys me. I miss my real dad a lot and only get to see him every other weekend. Tony will never be my dad and I wish he'd stop trying to interfere in my life. How can I get him to understand that?

Ryan, aged 11

magazine
Hobert

127 New Walk
Bringford

December 17

Dear Ryan
You don't say how long Tony has been living with you, but I would guess that it's not been long. It's not easy for Tony, either. It's really difficult to know how strict to be. The best way you can get him to stop being so strict is to try to be grown up. He will then see that you can be trusted and will give you more freedom.

Maggie, Agony Aunt

The Facts

Stepfamilies

✱ The number of stepfamilies is growing all the time—by 2010 there will be more stepfamilies than first families.

✱ Most children start living in a stepfamily between the ages of four and ten years old.

✱ Some children live in a stepfamily all the time. Others live in a stepfamily part of the time, or visit their stepfamily on the weekends or during school vacations.

✱ It can take time to adjust to living in a stepfamily: sometimes it means more people sharing a house, and unfamiliar house rules. But it also means more people to do things with, and talk to.

Your Views

What can Ryan do to make life easier living with his stepdad?

How can Tony become more accepted by Ryan?

What's it like being a part of a stepfamily?

At first, when my stepdad and his children moved in it felt like our house had been invaded. But now we are starting to get along, and find things we enjoy doing together.

Lauren, aged 12

I like staying with my dad and stepmom. I can tell my stepmom things I don't tell my mom.

Alex, aged 11

It really bugs me when my stepbrother calls my dad "dad," he's my dad, not his.

Nick, aged 10

I call him Chris. He's not my dad but we get along okay now. He's more like an uncle or something.

Michelle, aged 13

I can't live up to my brother

Hi Dan. Guess what. My brother was top of his class again.

Hi Conor. Hey u do alright u know!

My parents don't think so. He's always best. Footbl capt and everything.

U r lucky. I'd like a brother, not my stupid sister!

No way! Dale makes me feel a loser! Who needs brothers?

Conor's diary

19 August

Dale got his exam results today—brilliant as usual. I really hate him. Mom and Dad took us out for a celebration meal—guess I'll never have a celebration meal. I'll never be as good as him. He's better than me at everything.

Top Tips

Having talented brothers or sisters

⭐ Build your self-esteem by developing skills and interests of your own. Don't try to compete with siblings at their best subjects or sports—learn something really different for yourself.

⭐ Don't measure yourself against anyone or anything except your own goals.

⭐ Write a list of things you can do well. It doesn't have to be school subjects, it could be things like being kind to people, or being able to laugh at yourself.

⭐ Write a list of things you wish you could do better—then think of ways to improve on them.

⭐ Don't be afraid to ask your sibling to help you with things they are good at—they are family!

Your Views

Has Conor got a point? How would you feel if you were him?

What's it like to have a brother or sister?

I had to wait ages before I had a TV in my room, and now my sister's got one and she's only nine. It's so unfair.

Naomi, aged 12

Whenever we have an argument or a fight, my brother goes crying to Mom and she always believes him. He gets away with anything just because he's the youngest.

Bradley, aged 13

My sister used to be annoying, but now I like having an older sister. She can tell me about stuff I don't want to ask Mom or Dad.

Jasmine, aged 13

My younger sister gets all my dad's attention. I get really sick of it sometimes.

Carl, aged 11

I feel caught in the middle

March 2

Just got back from Dad's. It's been three months since he moved in with Ria. I think I was a bit hard on her at first, I didn't think she'd be so nice. She is always encouraging Dad to take us out and do things. We went ice-skating and out for lunch today. We probably do more things together than we used to when Dad lived at home. As usual though it was awful when I got home. Mom kept asking me about Ria and how she and Dad are getting along. It's horrible and I don't know what to say. I know Mom is still upset by the divorce but I don't want to feel like I'm a spy when I'm at Dad's. I don't know what to say to her and now I feel guilty about enjoying the weekend with Dad and Ria.

March 16

Dad just dropped me off and I heard him and Mom having a big argument about me staying more often at his place. I wish they'd just deal with it. Mom keeps asking me who I want to live with, but I don't know what to say.

Top Tips

Coping with divorced parents

★ About one in four children has parents who are divorced. If you are one of them, look at your class and you probably won't be alone.

★ Divorce is hard on everyone in a family: it will take time to adjust to new relationships.

★ Don't bottle up your feelings— tell your parents how you are feeling or, if it's hard to talk to them, find someone you can trust to talk to.

★ Don't be afraid of saying if something makes you feel uncomfortable or if you feel you are being asked to take sides.

How do you cope with your parents' divorce?

I keep some of my stuff at my Dad's house so it feels a bit more like home when I stay there.

Becky, aged 11

Mom complains about Dad, then he complains about Mom, and sometimes I feel like I'm stuck in the middle.

Sasha, aged 13

They're still your parents, even though they don't love each other any more, they both still love you and you can still talk to them.

Sam, aged 12

I wish Mom and Dad would get back together but I know it's not going to happen. I suppose it was worse sitting on the stairs listening to them arguing all the time.

Melissa, aged 12

Your Views

What should Hannah say to her mom when she asks her about Ria? Are Hannah's parents right to ask her who she wants to live with?

I have to look after my mom

Sam's advice column
Sorted magazine
Cedar Bluffs

Dear Sam

I am worried about my mom because she may have to go into the hospital. Mom has depression and sometimes she can't cope at home. I end up doing quite a bit of stuff like shopping and ironing but I am used to that now. The hard thing is I don't feel I can talk to any of my friends about it because I don't think they'll understand. I like to stay at home when Mom isn't well to try and take her mind off things, but sometimes I just say I have been grounded because that's easier. I am worried how long Mom will have to be in the hospital and sometimes I worry that I might get sick too, because I don't know who would look after me.

Kyle, aged 13

256 Bridge Road
Yellowing

Dear Kyle,
Your mom's illness means that you have had to grow up fast—taking care of yourself and your mom. But it's important that you find time to do things for yourself, like having a social life. If you are finding it hard to keep up with schoolwork, you should tell a teacher so they know what is happening at home. Young carers often feel isolated from friends. Try to find someone you can talk to—it could be a friend, a teacher, your mom's doctor, or a relative. Also, find out if there is a young carer's project near you—they can give advice, offer free evening clubs, and sometimes one-to-one help.

Sam, Agony Uncle

The Facts
Young carers

✳ Surveys show there is a "hidden army" of young carers looking after a parents.

✳ Most young carers are aged between 12 and 14.

✳ Many young carers complain of being bullied at school and feel their responsibilities set them apart from their peers.

✳ A young carer may feel their peers at school are immature—they may feel worried their friends are not like them.

✳ Carers of all ages often have low self-esteem—it is important they do things to boost their self-esteem, such as spending time with friends and developing their own interests.

✳ Check out page 29 for more information and help.

Your Views

Should Kyle try to tell his friends what is happening at home? What can he say to help them understand how he feels?

I still miss grandma

From: leanne@w███████.com
To: sarah_agonyaunt@█████████om
Date: Tuesday, March 7
Subject: I'm so sad

Dear Sarah

It's six months since grandma died. I still find it so hard without her. We were really close because I used to go to her house after school when my mom was at work. Now I go to an after-school club but I miss her so much. I could talk to her about anything. She was a really good listener, and she told me lots of stuff about when she was my age. She was the coolest person. She was funny and strong and caring and I find it really hard when I think about when she got sick. I hated seeing her in the hospital. I feel awful because I didn't go see her the week she died. She was so kind, and she did so much for me. I just feel really empty inside.

Leanne, aged 11

From: sarah_agonyaunt@████████om
To: leanne@w██████████.com
Date: Friday, March 10
Subject: Re: I'm so sad

Dear Leanne,

Losing someone close to us is one of the hardest things we go through—it happens to us all at some time. The more we love someone, the more it hurts when they die. The pain you are feeling is because you had such a strong relationship with your grandma. Don't keep your feelings bottled up. It may help to talk to a bereavement counselor—they know what you are going through and can support you. Try talking to your grandma as if she was still there—maybe find a quiet place where you feel you can talk aloud to her, or try writing your feelings down. Many people find themselves feeling guilty about something they did or didn't do or say before their loved one died. Don't worry about not seeing her before she died. You can be sure your grandma knew how much you loved her—and she will always be there in your memory every time you think of her.

Sarah, Agony Aunt

How do you cope with losing a loved one?

> The best advice I was given was to take things one day at a time. If you can get through today, that's enough.
>
> Danielle, aged 12

> When my sister died, I wrote a poem for her and we tied it to a balloon. Then we let the balloon go—it was like saying goodbye.
>
> Keeley, aged 13

Your Views

What could Leanne do to help her get over her grandma's death? How could her family and friends help her?

> When grandad died, we put a few things that reminded us of him in a shoebox. Mom said we can take out the box and remember him whenever we want to.
>
> Asema, aged 10

15

I don't like the way he looks at me

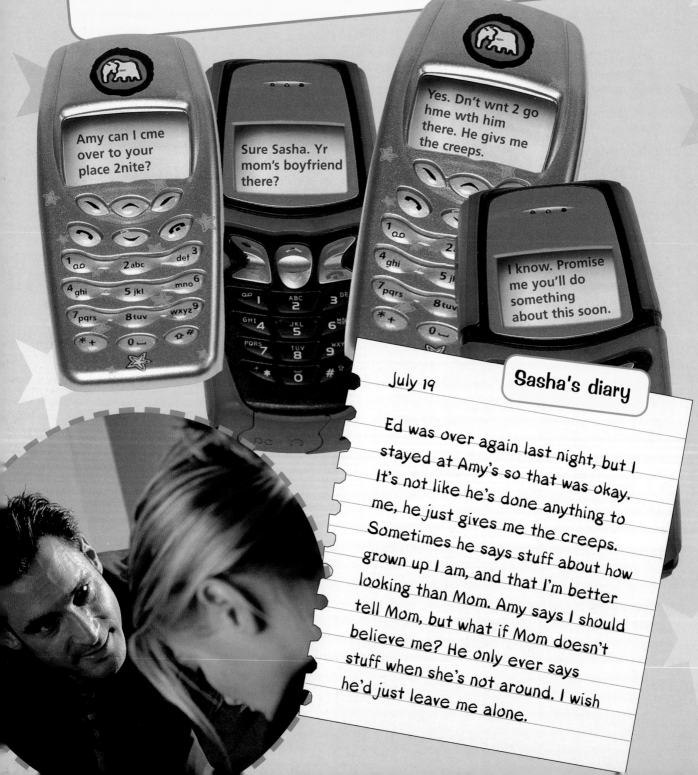

Amy can I cme over to your place 2nite?

Sure Sasha. Yr mom's boyfriend there?

Yes. Dn't wnt 2 go hme wth him there. He givs me the creeps.

I know. Promise me you'll do something about this soon.

Sasha's diary

July 19

Ed was over again last night, but I stayed at Amy's so that was okay. It's not like he's done anything to me, he just gives me the creeps. Sometimes he says stuff about how grown up I am, and that I'm better looking than Mom. Amy says I should tell Mom, but what if Mom doesn't believe me? He only ever says stuff when she's not around. I wish he'd just leave me alone.

The Facts

Abuse

❊ Forcing someone to do things they don't want to, touching or talking to them in a way that upsets them or makes them uncomfortable are all forms of abuse.

❊ Abusers are not usually strangers: they can be family members or friends.

❊ Abusers often build friendship and trust first; it can be confusing when they appear kind and caring in other ways.

Being abused leads to unhappiness, confusion, and maybe even feelings of guilt. But the abuser is the only one to blame: abuse is always wrong.

It is important to tell on an abuser, even if they try to make you keep their secret. Abuse has to be stopped and the abuser may need help too.

Top Tips

What can you do if you are abused?

★ Trust your own feelings—if you feel the way someone is behaving toward you is wrong, tell an adult you can trust, like a teacher.

★ Don't keep worries about abuse to yourself. There are helplines to call if you are feeling alone (see page 29).

★ If you think someone is abusing you in any way, tell them firmly you don't like it and you don't want them to do it again.

★ Take steps to try to make sure that you are never left alone with someone who makes you feel uncomfortable.

Your Views

Should Sasha tell her mom or someone else? Why might it be hard for Sasha to talk to her mom about this?

We argue all the time

From: Kelly-_Wills@█████████████om
To: mel21@████████████om
Date: Friday, July 15
Subject: Mom is driving me nuts!

Hi Mel

Can I stay over at your place tomorrow? I"m going nuts here. All I seem to do at home is argue with Mom. She is constantly on my case. It starts the moment I get up, "You're not going out dressed like that," or "Eat this, you need a good breakfast blah, blah," when I'm not even hungry! I wish she'd just realize it's my life, and let me get on with it. It never used to be like this. We used to get on okay. Now we argue about everything—it's like she can't accept I'm not a little kid any more. We had a big fight last night over the stupidest thing —I can't even remember how it started. It just kicked off and she said her classic, "I don't know who you are any more" and I said some pretty horrible things back. Why does she nag me all the time?

Anyway, I'll shut up for now. Let me know about tomorrow ASAP! :-)

Kelly

Item ID:
33357003747552
Call number: J 306.85
P871
Title: Me and my family
Author: Powell, Jillian.
Transit to: WESTBEND
Current time:
11/11/2008,17:39

What do you argue about with your parents?

My dad never shuts up about my cellphone bill and how long I've spent on the Internet. Don't they want me to have friends?

Raj, aged 12

If I'm watching one of my favorite programs, they say, "How can you watch that garbage?'

Kerry, aged 12

My mom is constantly nagging me about my room. She calls it the flea pit! If I'm happy the way it is, what's her problem?

Matt, aged 11

Homework. Money. Clothes. Those are the things we argue about—it's the same old stuff every time.

Janine, aged 13

Top Tips
Arguments with parents

★ Think about the reason for the argument: is it worth falling out about?

★ Don't end up insulting each other—you will both feel worse.

★ Say how you feel but try to think of the other person's feelings too—even when someone is giving you a hard time, it may be with the best intentions.

★ Don't bring up other issues—it only makes an argument worse.

★ Slow down your breathing and don't shout—you'll get a point across better if you stay calm.

Your Views

Why do you think things have changed between Kelly and her mom when they used to get along? Does it matter if you say horrible things to your family?

19

Mom doesn't have time for me now

115 Silver Street
Richmond

Hi Sunita

Sorry I haven't written lately—lousy penpal aren't I? How are things with you? I'm really tired of my new baby sister. It's like Kerry rules our lives, even though she's only tiny. I hate the way she's changed everything. She cries all the time and gives me a headache. Mom's always too busy or too tired to do stuff—she never wants to go shopping like we used to. Now Dad says we can't go abroad like we did last year because it's too hard taking a baby. The worst thing is I don't feel I can tell anyone how I feel because they all just say, "Aren't you lucky to have a baby sister?" But how can I love her when she has messed everything up?

Do you feel the same about your kid brother? Got to go, Mom's calling me. I promise to write more next time!

Luv Bethany

115 Silver St
Rich

Feb

227B Chancellor Street
Amherst

Hi Bethany

I know how you feel. I felt left out when Sanjay was born. Then Mom talked to me and said she really needed my help with the baby. I learned to feed him and change him and everything. Now Sanjay's a toddler, he's into everything. He's a real laugh—always up to something. I wouldn't be without him now and I think you will feel like that about Kerry one day. You'll be her big sister, and she will look up to you. In fact, I envy you having a sister. My mom is close to her sisters and I think it's lovely to have such great friends in your life.

Cheer up. Write soon. Sunita x

What's it like having a baby in the family?

> It was a weird feeling when Mom said, "Meet your baby brother," and I was a bit scared to hold him at first. Then he squeezed my finger, like he was saying hello!
>
> Ali, aged 13

> Babies get interesting when they start to talk. You know they are trying to copy what you say, and it's a nice feeling when you show them how to do things.
>
> Kirsty, aged 11

> I liked my sister when she was a baby, but now she's just annoying.
>
> Tom, aged 12

Your Views

What should Bethany do? What could her parents do to help her get used to having a baby around?

I can't help wondering about my real mom

Sam's advice column
Sorted magazine
Cedar Bluffs

Dear Sam

I've always known I was adopted. Mom and Dad told me everything to help me understand why my birth mom had to have me adopted. The trouble is lately I have started thinking a lot about my birth mom. I can't help wondering what she looks like and where she's living. I wonder if she thinks about me too. She might be famous or something—I even dream about that sometimes. Sometimes I feel I would like to meet her but I am worried about my mom and dad. They have always been great and I don't want to do anything to hurt them.

Martin, aged 13

Martin's diary

January 25

We did genes in biology today and how you get your eye color and stuff from your parents. Someone said something about having the same color hair as his grandma, and I felt a bit strange because I don't know what my real birth parents or my grandparents look like.

412 Mill Lane
Beamsville

Dear Martin,

It is natural to be curious about your birth family. Some people feel they need to learn about their roots to feel comfortable with who they are.

Tracing a birth family is a big step even when you are an adult. Adoption agencies will put you in touch with counselors to support you. Sometimes people find that their birth parents don't want to meet them, or have died. This can be emotionally upsetting. It's natural that your parents will feel unsettled too, but you can reassure them by talking to them about your own feelings and worries, and letting them know how important they are to you.

Sam, Agony Uncle

How does it feel to be adopted?

I know a lot of people feel they want to find out more, but I have never felt I wanted to contact my birth mother. My adoptive parents are my real parents to me. They are my mom and dad. I don't want anyone else.

Philippa, aged 12

I've got so many questions I want to ask. It's really scary, wondering what my birth mom is like, and whether she will want to meet me, but it's something I need to do.

Siobhan, aged 13

When Mom told me I was adopted I felt a bit upset. It doesn't feel as bad now, knowing my mom wanted me so much.

Ricky, aged 12

Your Views

Do you think Martin should try to meet his birth mother? What are the pros and cons?

I get no privacy

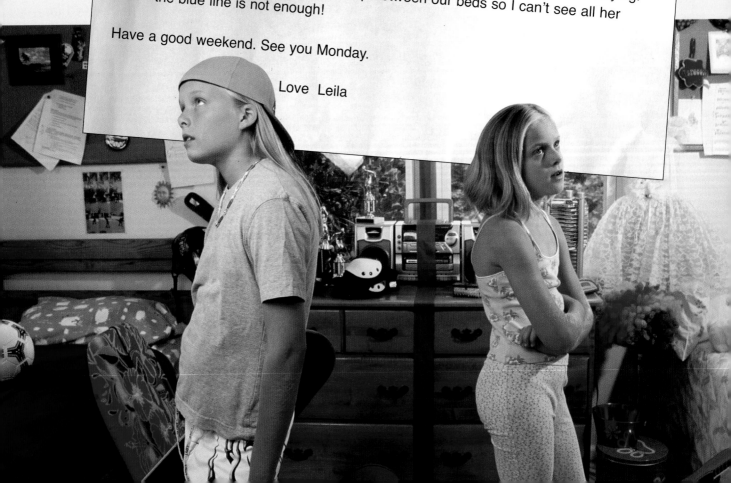

From: leila243@an▓▓▓▓▓▓▓▓▓▓▓
To: deborah.steele@▓▓▓▓▓▓▓▓▓m
Date: Saturday, April 3
Subject: That nosy sister again!

Dear Debs

Thanks for calling me on my cell. I thought I'd send you a quick email to say sorry I couldn't say much. As usual, Megan was listening in. I hate sharing my bedroom with her. It's so unfair. Tom gets to have a room on his own, and I have to share with her. She's so nosy it's driving me crazy. She's not interested in clothes or anything, all she talks about is football—it's so boring! I think we will have to invent a secret code or something! I can't have my friends over or anything, because she's so annoying. I'm going to ask Mum to put a screen up between our beds so I can't see all her stuff—the blue line is not enough!

Have a good weekend. See you Monday.

Love Leila

Top Tips

Sharing a bedroom

★ If you have to share a bedroom, try negotiating so you each have a little time every week when the room is just yours. Hang a "Do not disturb" sign on the door.

★ Keep a secret diary with a lock, where you can write down your thoughts and ideas.

★ Libraries are good places for quiet time. Reading helps you escape into another world.

★ Sharing means twice as much mess: make sure you have a system so you take turns tidying—having clutter around will make you both stressed.

Your Views

Why do you think sharing a room is often annoying for teenagers? What could the sisters do to make it easier?

Do you like sharing a room?

I suppose the best thing about sharing is we get to have bunks. Especially since I grabbed the top one!

Ethan, aged 12

Sharing a room with my sister isn't too bad. We often lie awake and talk for ages when Mom and Dad think we're asleep!

Nicola, aged 10

I wish I had more space sometimes. It's hard keeping a room tidy when there are two of you sharing. My brother is always complaining about my music too, which is a total pain.

Ali, aged 11

They are always making me do chores

Sam's advice column
Sorted magazine
Cedar Bluffs

Dear Sam

Why do my parents treat me like I am six years old? My mom nags me to do stuff at home when I want to be out with my friends. I am only allowed out one night a week and then I have to be in by the time they say. If I am just a bit late getting back, I get grounded. It's really embarrassing and my friends are starting to give me a hard time about it. I am always being grounded for something, or given stupid punishments like having to clean out the hamster's cage or taking out the garbage for a week. I've tried saying that I'm not a kid any more but they just say, "While you are under our roof you'll do as we say." That just makes me want to move out!

Craig, aged 14

September 28

643 Rushey Vale
Seneca Falls

Dear Craig

It's sometimes hard for parents to adjust to their children growing up and changing so fast. They need to know you still want to spend time with them at home, and don't want to feel they are losing you to your friends. The secret is negotiation. You need to show your parents that you are happy to spend some time at home, and to pull your weight by helping out—it's only right to share the chores. Getting used to helping run a home will give you a head start for when you do move away and get your own place. The key is communication: you need to show your parents you can act responsibly, then you can negotiate a bit more freedom.

Sam, Agony Uncle

How do you get along with your parents?

I always seem to get the boring stuff to do in our house because I am the youngest and everyone feels they can boss me around.
Danny, aged 9

We have these family pow wows once a week, and everyone gets to have their say. I thought they were stupid at first, but at least you can air things that are bugging you.
Melanie, aged 12

Some of my friends get given rewards for passing exams and stuff. It's really unfair—my parents just expect me to do well anyway.
Devra, aged 11

Your Views

What's the best way for Craig to persuade his parents that he should have more freedom?

Glossary

Abuse
Hurting someone by words or actions that make them feel unhappy or distressed, or forcing them to do things they do not want to do.

Bereavement
The feeling of loss when someone you love dies.

Birth family/parents
The natural or biological family or parents.

Depression
When someone feels low and unhappy and the feelings don't go away. Depression can be an illness that needs treatment.

Divorce
When two people who are married part and their marriage is ended by law.

Genes
Part of our physical make-up that contains our DNA and passes on characteristics from our parents.

Negotiation
Discussion so that two or more people or groups can agree on something.

Peers
People of the same age group.

Self-esteem
How we feel and think about ourselves.

Sibling
A brother or sister.

Stepfamily
A family formed when two people decide to live together, and one or both bring a child from a previous marriage.

Young carer
Someone who takes on the responsibility of caring for a relative, and sometimes a home, when they are still a child or teenager.

Websites

www.familydoctor.org
Go to Parents & Kids and then click on Dealing with Feelings. Here you will find large number of articles about the home and family, thoughts and feelings, and emotions and behavior.

www.gmrdesign.com/ lifechallenges.org
A website that can be accessed any time, day or night, when you need support dealing with any life challenges, such as illness, relationship/family issues, and dealing with death and grief.

www.rethink.org/
A website devoted to the mental health of young people and children. Type any subject, for example, "self harm" into the site's search engine for information, support , and articles.

www.childrenssociety.org.uk/ youngcarers
Offers information and support for young carers and their families.

www.people-search.com/ adoptionsearch.htm
This website offers a worldwide adoption-search database.

www.focusas.com/Hotlines.html
This site provides hotlines and helplines for a wide range of support organizations, such as Alcoholics Anonymous and Alateen Family Group, National Domestic Violence Hotline, and the National Hopeline Network, as well as many others.

www.childhelpus.org
Childhelp is one of the largest and oldest national, nonprofit organizations dedicated to the treatment, prevention and research of child abuse and neglect. Their website offers a national hotline that victims of child abuse can ring for support.

www.nspcc.org.uk
Website of a charity that campaigns against cruelty to children. It includes information on family problems and a helpline to ring.

Index

abuse 16, 17, 28, 29
adoption 22, 23, 29
arguing 10, 11, 18, 19

babies 20, 21
bereavement 14, 15, 28, 29
birth parents 22, 23, 28

counselors 15, 23

dads 6, 7, 8, 9, 10, 11, 19, 20, 22, 23, 25
death 14, 15
depression 12, 28
divorce 10, 11, 29

friends 12, 13, 15, 17, 19

growing up 26, 27

moms 6, 7, 8, 9, 10, 11, 12, 13, 14, 15, 16, 17, 18, 19, 20, 21, 22, 23, 25, 26

parents 8, 11, 19, 21, 22, 23, 26, 27

self-esteem 9, 13, 28
sharing a room 24, 25
sibling rivalry 8, 9
stepdads 6, 7
stepfamilies 7, 10, 28

young carers 12, 13

This edition first published in 2008 by
Sea-to-Sea Publications
1980 Lookout Drive
North Mankato
Minnesota 56003

Copyright © Sea-to-Sea Publications 2008

Printed in China

All rights reserved.

Library of Congress Cataloging in Publication Data

Powell, Jillian.
  Me and my family / by Jillian Powell.
    p.cm. -- (Problem page)
  Includes index.
  ISBN 978-1-59771-088-6
  1. Family--Juvenile literature. 2. Communication in the family--Juvenile
literature. 3. Parent and child--Juvenile literature. I. Title.

HQ744.P69 2007
306.85--dc22

2006053104

9 8 7 6 5 4 3 2

Published by arrangement with the Watts Publishing
Group Ltd, London.

Series editor: Sarah Peutrill
Art director: Jonathan Hair
Design: Rita Storey
Picture researcher: Diana Morris
Advisor: Wendy Anthony, Health education
consultant

Picture credits: Alix/Phanie/Rex Features: 14. Paul
Baldesare/Photofusion: 12. John Birdsall Photography:
6, 7, 27. Burger/Phanie/Rex Features: 9t.
Comstock/Alamy: 11. Dex Images/Corbis: front cover t,
24. Sarah Flanagan/Rex Features: 8b. Gina
Glover/Photofusion: 22. Image Works/Topham: 18.
Alistair Linford/Alamy: 23. Brian Mitchell/Photofusion:
17. Maggie Murray/Photofusion: 26. Pictor/Alamy: 16b.
John Powell/Topham: front cover b, 3, 19. Ulrike
Preuss/Photofusion: 13, 25.
Lynne Siler/Focus Group/Alamy: 20.
Voisin/Phanie/Rex Features: 10. David Wogan/Alamy:
15.

Every attempt has been made to clear copyright.
Should there be any inadvertent omission please apply
to the publisher for rectification. All photos posed by
models.